THE WHEELCHAIR WARRIORS'
BIBLE

BY: TAMMY L BROWN

For Rocky

"The Wheelchair Warrior's Bible"

Exposing Inaccessibility

Despite ADA Laws

INTRODUCTION

In the pages that follow, allow me to introduce myself as Tammy Brown, an author whose personal journey has been deeply shaped by the challenges and triumphs of navigating a world that often falls short of providing equitable accessibility for individuals with disabilities. My story unfolds against the backdrop of a unique partnership—I am married to a combat-disabled veteran who relies on a wheelchair for mobility. Together, we have embarked on numerous journeys, both near and far, seeking the enriching experiences that travel can offer. However, our adventures have been punctuated by a recurring, disheartening obstacle: the pervasive lack of adequate wheelchair accessibility. As I too rely on a mobility device, our shared quest for exploration often finds us separated, each confined to a different vehicle due to the limitations of accommodating multiple wheelchairs. In these moments, we have encountered well-meaning individuals who, while striving to adhere to the minimum requirements established by the Americans with Disabilities Act (ADA), inadvertently overlook the essence of accessibility and the challenges that persist for those of us living with disabilities.

The Americans with Disabilities Act (ADA), a landmark piece of legislation enacted in 1990, embodies a profound promise of inclusion and equal opportunities for individuals with disabilities across the United States. This transformative law pledges to eliminate discrimination because of disability in various aspects of public life, ranging from employment and public accommodations to transportation and telecommunications. Through its comprehensive framework, the ADA seeks to break down barriers, promote accessibility, and ensure that people with disabilities can fully participate in society. It stands as a beacon of hope and progress, reaffirming the commitment to a more equitable and accessible future for all, regardless of their physical or cognitive abilities. These are noble causes I'm sure implemented with pure intent. They look great on paper and make excellent talking points, but how well do they really work for the Disabled community? This narrative chronicles our journey through these encounters, shedding light on the subtle yet profound ways in which we can bridge the gap between compliance and true inclusivity and provides the essential tools for bringing those that are non-compliant to justice!

Chapter 1: The Promise of ADA

In the summer of 1990, a historic moment unfolded in the United States Congress, a moment that would forever change the lives of millions of Americans living with disabilities. It was the birth of the Americans with Disabilities Act (ADA), a watershed piece of legislation that emerged from years of grassroots activism, advocacy, and unwavering determination.

The ADA's origins can be traced back to the tireless efforts of disability rights activists, who fought for recognition and equal rights in a society that often marginalized and excluded them. Their voices, led by remarkable figures like Justin Dart and Judith Heumann, echoed through the halls of Congress, demanding justice, dignity, and accessibility for all.

The ADA's primary goal was clear: to combat discrimination against individuals with disabilities in all facets of public life. It sought to eliminate barriers to employment, ensuring that people with disabilities would have equal opportunities to work and contribute to society. It demanded accessible public spaces, transportation, and communication, making the world more navigable for those with mobility, sensory, or cognitive impairments.

This groundbreaking legislation was designed to foster a society where disability was not a hindrance but a facet of diversity to be embraced. It aimed to create a culture of inclusion, where everyone, regardless of their abilities, could participate fully in the social, economic, and political life of the nation.

The birth of the ADA was a testament to the power of collective action, a reminder that progress could be achieved when people came together to champion a just cause. Its goals were not merely legal; they were aspirations for a more compassionate and accessible world, where the promise of equality would extend to all, regardless of their physical or cognitive differences.

As the ADA became law, it marked a turning point in American history, setting a standard for disability rights that would inspire similar legislation worldwide. Its legacy endures, reminding us that the pursuit of a more inclusive society is a noble and ongoing endeavor—one that requires vigilance, compassion, and unwavering commitment to the principles that birthed this remarkable legislation. The ADA remains a beacon of hope, a symbol of progress, and a reminder that when we work together for the common good, we can break down barriers and make the world a better place for all its citizens.

In its initial years, the ADA had a profound impact on employment opportunities for people with disabilities. Employers were now required to provide reasonable accommodation to ensure that qualified individuals with disabilities could perform their job duties effectively. This shift in workplace culture allowed many talented individuals to join the workforce, contributing their skills and expertise to various industries.

Public accommodations also saw transformative changes. Restaurants, stores, theaters, and other businesses underwent renovations to become more accessible, ensuring that individuals with mobility impairments could enter and enjoy their services without obstacles. The iconic curb cuts and ramps that now grace sidewalks across the nation became a symbol of this newfound accessibility.

The ADA also influenced the design of transportation systems. Buses and trains were modified to accommodate wheelchairs and individuals with disabilities, making public transportation more inclusive. Air travel, too, saw improvements, with regulations requiring airlines to provide accessible seating and services.

The realm of telecommunications witnessed advancements as well. The ADA's Title IV mandated the establishment of the Telecommunications Relay Service (TRS), which enabled individuals with hearing and speech disabilities to communicate over the telephone using relay operators. This innovation vastly improved communication and accessibility for this segment of the population.

Over the years, the ADA's reach expanded. The law extended its protections to the digital realm, requiring websites and online services to be accessible to individuals with disabilities. This adaptation reflected the evolving nature of technology and its growing importance in modern life.

The ADA's successes were not without challenges, and progress has been ongoing. Advocates and organizations tirelessly work to ensure that the law is upheld and that new challenges, such as those posed by evolving technologies, are addressed. Additionally, the ADA has influenced global attitudes toward disability rights, serving as a model for similar legislation in countries around the world.

While significant strides have been made since its inception, the ADA's mission continues. It reminds us that the journey toward full inclusion and accessibility is ongoing, requiring collective effort, awareness, and dedication to the principles of equity and equal opportunity. The ADA's early successes paved the way for a more inclusive society, and its legacy inspires us to keep pushing boundaries and advancing the cause of disability rights.

In the ever-evolving tapestry of society, the ongoing battle for equal access for disabled people is a silent revolution, an unwavering quest to break down barriers, both physical and societal. This is a story of collective determination, resilience, and the enduring spirit of a community that refuses to be confined by limitations.

In cities and towns, across nations and continents, a diverse spectrum of individuals with disabilities navigates a world that often falls short of being fully inclusive. From wheelchair users seeking access to public transportation to the blind who yearn for information in accessible formats, their stories are as varied as the challenges they face. Yet, their common thread is the shared aspiration for a world where their disabilities do not define their limitations.

The battle for equal access unfolds on many fronts. It begins with the physical environment, where ramps, elevators, and accessible facilities transform seemingly insurmountable obstacles into manageable challenges. It extends to transportation, where accessible buses, trains, and stations become lifelines to independence and mobility.

But this battle transcends the concrete and steel of infrastructure. It delves deep into the heart of society, where attitudes, prejudices, and misconceptions create barriers that are often invisible but profoundly restrictive. The disabled community, joined by allies and advocates, tirelessly challenges these stereotypes, advocating for acceptance, inclusion, and equal opportunities.

Education becomes a pivotal battleground. In classrooms, lecture halls, and libraries, disabled students demand the right to learn on equal terms. The battle for accessible educational materials, supportive services, and inclusive curricula wages on, ensuring that knowledge becomes a beacon that shines for all.

In workplaces, disabled individuals champion their skills and talents, striving for careers that align with their aspirations and capabilities. Employers are urged to dismantle preconceived notions, offering reasonable accommodations that enable disabled workers to thrive and contribute to their fullest potential.

The digital realm, a relatively new frontier, emerges as both a battleground and a tool of empowerment. Web accessibility standards are forged, ensuring that the internet, the great equalizer of our age, remains open to all, regardless of disability. Online communities flourish, connecting people with shared experiences and aspirations, creating a powerful platform for change.

While battles are won, new challenges arise, for the journey towards equal access is an ongoing one. Legislation and policies evolve to reflect the changing needs of the disabled community, driven by their voices and demands. Through marches, protests, advocacy, and dialogue, the battle remains at the forefront of societal consciousness.

The disabled community, bound together by the unwavering belief in their rights, persists in their fight. Their collective voice grows stronger with each victory, each change in perception, each inch of progress. They are warriors of resilience, agents of transformation, and champions of inclusion.

In the end, the story of the ongoing battle for equal access for disabled people is not just a narrative; it is a testament to the human spirit's boundless capacity for resilience and progress. It is a reminder that a world built on the principles of equity, empathy, and inclusivity benefits not only the disabled community but all of humanity. The battle continues, driven by the shared vision of a more accessible and inclusive world, where everyone can thrive, regardless of their abilities.

Chapter 2: The Reality of Inaccessibility

Every day, for those who navigate life from a wheelchair, the world unfolds as a tapestry of challenges and triumphs, a journey marked by resilience, determination, and a profound sense of self-reliance.

Alex...

Meet Alex, a young woman whose indomitable spirit defies the limitations of her wheelchair. Each morning, her day begins with the mechanical hum of her electric wheelchair coming to life. As she rolls out of her bedroom, the world outside her window awaits, full of possibilities and obstacles.

The first challenge, one that most people take for granted, is the simple act of getting dressed. For Alex, it requires a deliberate and skillful process, often involving adaptive clothing and assistive devices. With patience and precision, she transforms herself into the vibrant individual she knows herself to be.

Navigating her home, which she has thoughtfully designed to be wheelchair accessible, is a matter of ease. Ramps and widened doorways, strategically placed grab bars, and a customized kitchen allow her to maintain her independence. Technology, a trusty ally, helps her control lights, appliances, and security systems with a tap on her tablet.

As she ventures out into the world, the landscape changes. The urban environment, though increasingly accommodating, presents its own set of challenges. Sidewalks often prove to be obstacle courses, with uneven surfaces, cracked pavements, and curbs that are either missing or too high. But Alex, a seasoned navigator, deftly maneuvers her chair, using ramps or seeking assistance from kind-hearted strangers when needed.

Public transportation, a lifeline for many, remains a mixed bag of accessibility. Buses equipped with ramps or low-floor designs are a welcome sight, but she must always check schedules and routes to ensure a smooth journey. Train stations with elevators become her gateways to adventure, granting her access to the heart of the city and beyond.

Shopping, once an enjoyable outing, is now a strategic mission. Alex must consider store layouts, aisles wide enough to accommodate her chair, and accessible fitting rooms. She often finds herself enlisting the help of store employees to reach items placed on high shelves, transforming shopping into a communal experience.

At work, where she's a dedicated graphic designer, Alex's talents shine brightly. Her desk is equipped with a height-adjustable workstation, enabling her to create artistry with ease. Colleagues are accommodating, and the company has embraced a culture of inclusion. Yet, she occasionally confronts the barriers of corporate culture, the unspoken assumptions that limit her opportunities.

Amid these daily challenges, Alex is acutely aware of the moments of triumph that punctuate her journey. The joy of an accessible park, where she can savor the tranquility of nature. The warmth of friendships forged through shared experiences. The exhilaration of dancing at an inclusive event, where she's not defined by her chair but celebrated for her spirit.

Navigating daily life as a wheelchair user is a unique journey, filled with both hurdles and victories. It's a life of adapting, problem-solving, and discovering the profound strength within. Through every twist and turn, Alex and countless others like her remind us that the human spirit is capable of transcending limitations, and that the world, as it becomes more accessible, holds boundless opportunities for all who dare to roll forward with courage and determination.

But what does one do in situations that are not as accommodating?

Larry...

In a gleaming, state-of-the-art casino, nestled within the depths of a restroom, a comical misadventure was about to unfold, starring none other than Larry – a handicapped gentleman with a penchant for adventure and a wheelchair that had an affinity for tight spaces.

Larry had ventured into the restroom, not anticipating that this would be the day he'd find himself in a jam of truly epic proportions. He rolled into the ADA-compliant, spacious handicapped stall, which, on the surface, seemed like a haven for wheelchair users. Little did he know it would soon become a labyrinthine trap that not even a maze-loving hamster would envy.

Larry, always one to see the glass as half full, cheerily announced to his wheelchair, "Here we are, buddy! The high roller's suite!" But as he attempted to exit the stall, he realized that luxury had its own quirks.

His wheelchair, typically obedient, appeared to have developed a stubborn streak. It was as if it had decided to park itself in a spot so tight that Houdini himself would've raised an eyebrow. In the confined space between the wall and the toilet, his beloved wheelchair had staged a coup.

With a befuddled expression that quickly transformed into amusement, Larry muttered, "Well, isn't this just the jackpot of predicaments?" He attempted to perform a series of acrobatics that would make a contortionist envious, twisting and turning in his seat to extricate himself from the clutches of the restroom stall.

With every twist and turn, Larry's trusty wheels remained resolutely immobile, as though they had gone on strike. He couldn't help but imagine his wheelchair whispering to itself, "Larry needs to hold onto his winnings just a little bit longer; let's help him out!"

Realizing that he was not going to outmaneuver this wily bathroom stall with sheer willpower, Larry decided to call for help. With a dramatic flair that would make Shakespeare proud, he bellowed, "Hark, kind stranger! I am ensnared in the clutches of this treacherous stall!"

A fellow restroom-goer, intrigued by the dramatic performance, knocked on the stall door. Larry recounted his comedic plight, explaining how even an agile cat would've struggled to escape the grasp of this bathroom stall.

Together, they hatched a brilliant escape plan. With teamwork that would have made NASA engineers proud, they skillfully pivoted, wiggled, and maneuvered the wheelchair until, finally, it broke free from its porcelain prison.

As Larry emerged from the stall, he couldn't resist one last quip, "Well, they say the most successful casinos are theme based, but these guys took it to an entirely different level – even the bathroom stalls are like the slots – enticing me to 'take a seat' with all their bells and whistles then trying to prevent me from leaving!"

The kind stranger, now in stitches from Larry's dry humor, gave him a hearty pat on the back before going on his merry way.

Larry wheeled himself out of the restroom, determined to remember this bathroom stall escapade as one of life's comical detours. He knew that even in the tightest spots, a dash of humor could help him roll right through any situation, even if it meant momentarily getting tangled up in a restroom stall's mystifying web.

A funny story where many of us can relate, but are we really using humor just to mask the frustration and embarrassment? Surely in the 21st century with all the ADA requirements this is the exception and not the rule, right?

Unfortunately, these things happen far more often than they should, complements of merchants and corporate ownership that strive to meet the "minimum requirements" to become compliant.

Linda and Robert…

In the quiet corners of their home, Linda watched her husband, Robert, who had once been a proud soldier, move through life in a wheelchair, his eyes betraying a mix of frustration, longing, and a profound sense of loss. The emotional toll of inaccessibility weighed heavily on his broad shoulders, and she, as his unwavering partner, felt every ounce of it.

Robert had always been a man of unwavering independence and strength, both on the battlefield and in the everyday battles of life. But the day he found himself confined to a wheelchair, after an accident during his service, marked a profound shift in their world.

Linda remembered the early days when they both struggled to adapt. The tears and whispered conversations in the dead of night became the silent witnesses to their shared pain. As Robert's wheelchair became his new companion, Linda saw him wrestle with the emotions of reliance on others, a stark contrast to the self-sufficient soldier he once was.

The emotional toll was most evident in the countless outings that ended in frustration and disappointment. The places they had once enjoyed as an able-bodied couple were now fortresses of inaccessibility. The steep curbs, narrow doorways, and flights of stairs transformed what should have been simple errands into insurmountable obstacles.

One particularly poignant memory was their attempt to visit a local restaurant for their anniversary. Linda had called ahead to inquire about accessibility, only to be met with an assurance that the restaurant was wheelchair friendly. But upon arrival, they discovered a small step at the entrance, an insurmountable barrier for Robert's wheelchair. The disappointment in his eyes, masked by a brave smile, cut through Linda's heart like a knife.

As Linda pushed Robert's wheelchair away from the inaccessible restaurant, she could sense his pride wrestling with the bitterness of dependence. He had served his country with honor, and now he found himself at the mercy of a world that often fell short in providing the basic accommodations he needed.

The emotional toll was not just about the physical limitations but also the subtle reminders of his changed circumstances. Friends who once sought his counsel and advice now saw him as the "disabled" friend, a label that grated against his self-esteem. The glances from strangers, sometimes filled with pity or discomfort, pierced through Robert's resilience.

Linda, however, was his rock. She watched him grieve the loss of mobility, the loss of freedom, and the loss of the life he had known. And as she held him through those moments of vulnerability, she marveled at his enduring spirit.

Together, they became advocates, not just for Robert but for countless others who faced similar challenges. They tirelessly spoke out against inaccessibility, urging businesses and communities to make the necessary changes. Robert's military discipline and Linda's unwavering support became a formidable force for change.

In the quiet moments, as they faced the emotional toll of inaccessibility together, Linda saw a transformation in Robert. He learned that asking for help did not diminish his strength but instead revealed the depth of his resilience. And though the world may have denied him certain physical freedoms, it had not dampened the fire of his spirit.

Their journey was not without its heartaches, but it was also filled with moments of triumph and a deepening bond that transcended physical limitations. Together, they discovered that the true measure of a person's strength lay not in their ability to stand alone but in their capacity to lean on others and, in doing so, forge an unbreakable connection built on love and resilience.

These personal stories are just a few examples of what living daily with physical and mental limitations can be like. There are millions of stories, from all walks of life, that are similar in one way or another to the few I have chosen for this book.Accumulated, these stories of small battles won, and larger wars still being fought, are the realities of inaccessibility.

Chapter 3: Misleading Claims and Compliance

The Americans with Disabilities Act (ADA) is a crucial piece of legislation designed to ensure equal access and opportunities for individuals with disabilities. ADA compliance is not just a legal requirement; it's a moral and ethical obligation for businesses to create inclusive environments. Unfortunately, some companies engage in deceptive practices by misleading their patrons and boasting about their ADA compliance when they fall short of the necessary standards. This deceptive behavior can have severe consequences, both legally and morally.

The Legal Framework

Before delving into specific cases, it's essential to understand the legal framework surrounding ADA compliance. The ADA prohibits discrimination against individuals with disabilities in all areas of public life, including employment, public accommodations, transportation, and government services. Public accommodations include businesses that are open to the public, such as hotels, restaurants, theaters, and retail stores just to name a few. To be ADA compliant, these businesses must ensure that their facilities are accessible to individuals with disabilities.

The Deceptive Practices

Inadequate Accessibility Features: Some companies claim ADA compliance while providing only superficial accommodations. For instance, they may install a wheelchair ramp but fail to ensure that it meets the required specifications, making it difficult or impossible for individuals using wheelchairs to access the premises. Similarly, restrooms may be labeled as ADA compliant, but they lack the proper grab bars, sink height, or space for wheelchair users.

False Certifications: In some cases, businesses obtain certificates or signs that suggest they are ADA compliant when they are not. These deceptive practices mislead patrons into believing they will have full access, only to face obstacles when they arrive.

Lack of Training: Companies may boast about their ADA compliance without adequately training their staff on how to assist individuals with disabilities. This can lead to unintentional discrimination or discomfort for disabled patrons.

Unlawful Denials: Some businesses claim ADA compliance but unlawfully deny entry or services to individuals with disabilities. This can include denying access to service animals or refusing to provide reasonable accommodations.

Case Studies

The Accessible Restaurant That Wasn't: A restaurant in a popular tourist destination proudly displayed an ADA-compliant sign on its front door. However, upon inspection, it was discovered that the restaurant lacked accessible seating, had a non-compliant bathroom, and staff members were unfamiliar with how to assist customers with disabilities. The restaurant faced legal consequences and had to undergo substantial renovations to become truly accessible.

The Hotel Chain Under Investigation: A well-known hotel chain faced allegations of falsely claiming ADA compliance across its properties. Investigations revealed that many of their locations had numerous violations, from inaccessible parking lots to poorly designed rooms. The company faced lawsuits and had to invest significant resources in upgrading its facilities.

The Consequences of Deceptive Claims

Legal Consequences: Companies that falsely claim ADA compliance can face legal action, including fines and settlements. These legal battles can damage a company's reputation and financial stability.

Reputation Damage: Misleading patrons about ADA compliance can result in significant damage to a company's reputation. Word-of-mouth, negative reviews, and social media backlash can deter potential customers and harm a business's bottom line.

Ethical Implications: Deceptive practices regarding ADA compliance are not just a legal issue but also an ethical one. They undermine the principles of equality and inclusion that the ADA seeks to uphold.

Misleading patrons and boasting about ADA compliance while failing to meet the necessary standards is not only unethical but also potentially illegal. Companies that engage in such practices risk legal consequences, damage to their reputation, and ethical scrutiny. It is essential for businesses to prioritize genuine ADA compliance, not only to avoid negative consequences but also to foster inclusivity and equal access for all members of the community. ADA compliance should be more than just a boast—it should be a sincere commitment to inclusivity and accessibility.

Where there is noncompliance, it is my wish that we, a self-appointed brigade of Wheelchair Warriors, expose them and hold them accountable for their discriminatory practices. But how can we go about exposing these injustices?

Step 1: Gather Information

Start by gathering information about the business in question. This includes details such as the business name, address, and any advertising or promotional material where accessibility claims are made. Note down any specific claims the business has made regarding its accessibility features.

Step 2: Conduct On-Site Inspections

If possible, visit the business in person to conduct an on-site inspection. Look for common accessibility features such as accessible parking spaces, ramps, door width, bathroom facilities, and signage. Document any discrepancies between the claimed accessibility and what you observe. Take pictures!

Step 3: Interview Patrons and Employees

Engage with patrons and employees of the business to gather information about their experiences regarding accessibility. Ask if they have encountered any challenges or noticed any false claims regarding accessibility features. Be respectful and empathetic when discussing these issues.

Step 4: Review Public Records

Check public records, such as building permits, inspection reports, and complaints filed against the business. These records can provide valuable insights into the business's compliance with accessibility standards and any past violations.

Step 5: Online Research

Explore the business's online presence, including their website and social media accounts. Look for any claims or statements related to accessibility. Take screenshots or save web pages for reference.

Step 6: Consult Accessibility Experts

Consider seeking advice from accessibility experts or disability rights organizations. They can provide guidance on identifying compliance issues and assessing the accuracy of accessibility claims.

Step 7: File Complaints with Authorities

If you have substantial evidence of false accessibility claims, consider filing complaints with the appropriate authorities. This may include local building code enforcement agencies, disability rights organizations, or the Department of Justice (DOJ) for ADA violations. Provide all your gathered evidence to support your complaint.

Step 8: Raise Public Awareness

Share your findings and experiences with the public through social media, blogs, or local media outlets. Raising awareness can put pressure on the business to rectify accessibility issues and can also serve as a warning to others who may encounter similar problems.

Step 9: Legal Action

In cases where false claims are persistent and severe, individuals or advocacy groups may consider legal action against the business. Consult with an attorney experienced in disability rights to explore your legal options.

Exposing false accessibility claims made by businesses is a crucial step in ensuring equal access and rights for individuals with disabilities. By following this step-by-step guide and filling out your fact-finding sheets in your Wheelchair Warriors Worksheets in the back of this book, you can play a vital role in holding businesses accountable for their actions and promoting a more inclusive society. Remember that transparency and collaboration with accessibility experts and advocacy groups can be powerful tools in your pursuit of justice and equality, but sometimes, as the saying goes, it's best to just take the bull by the horns.

To recap, uncovering hidden barriers related to ADA non-compliance by businesses requires a thorough and systematic approach. These hidden barriers may not be immediately obvious but can significantly impact the accessibility of a business for individuals with disabilities so get out there with this book and utilize the worksheets in the back and start documenting. Pictures, screenshots, and sometimes just having an honest conversation with a fellow patron or employee can sometimes unearth loads of pertinent information to further your cause. Remember – this is a war, and you are the consummate Wheelchair Warrior on the front lines!

Chapter 4: Navigating Public Spaces

Accessible parking spaces are a lifeline for individuals with disabilities, offering them the opportunity to participate fully in society. While these parking spots are mandated by laws such as the Americans with Disabilities Act (ADA) and various international regulations, the challenges of handicapped accessible parking persist. Let's explore the common challenges faced by individuals with disabilities when it comes to accessible parking and advocate for a more inclusive and equitable parking environment.

1. Insufficient Availability

One of the most pressing challenges in handicapped accessible parking is the limited availability of designated spaces. Many parking lots and facilities often allocate only the minimum number of accessible spots required by law. As a result, individuals with disabilities may struggle to find an open space, leading to inconvenience and potential barriers to accessing businesses and services.

2. Misuse and Abuse of Accessible Parking

Another significant issue is the misuse and abuse of accessible parking spaces by drivers who do not have disabilities. This behavior not only denies individuals with disabilities access to the parking they need but is also illegal and unethical. Some common forms of misuse include:

- Unauthorized vehicles parking in accessible spaces.
- Using a handicapped placard or license plate that doesn't belong to the driver.
- Parking in access aisles or curb cuts, blocking ramp access.

Addressing this challenge requires increased vigilance and enforcement of parking regulations, as well as public education on the importance of accessible parking spaces.

3. Poorly Designed Accessible Spaces

While having accessible parking spaces is essential, the design and maintenance of these spaces are equally crucial. Inadequate striping, faded paint, or improperly marked signage can create confusion and make it difficult for individuals with disabilities to identify accessible spots. Additionally, some parking lots have poorly designed access aisles or ramps that are not up to code, making it challenging for wheelchair users and those with mobility aids to navigate.

4. Inadequate Access Aisles and Pathways

Access aisles are meant to provide space for wheelchair users to exit and enter their vehicles comfortably. However, these areas are often blocked by other vehicles, shopping carts, or debris. Even a slight obstruction can make it impossible for someone with a disability to use the accessible parking space effectively.

5. Distance from Amenities

In some cases, accessible parking spaces are located a considerable distance from the entrance of a building or facility. This can pose a significant challenge for individuals with limited mobility, making it exhausting and time-consuming to reach their destination. Businesses and public spaces should aim to place accessible parking spaces as close as possible to entrances and amenities.

6. Lack of Enforcement and Accountability

While regulations exist to protect accessible parking spaces, enforcement can be lax, leaving violators unpunished. Strengthening enforcement measures and holding those who misuse accessible parking accountable is crucial in addressing this challenge.

Handicapped accessible parking is more than just convenience; it's a fundamental aspect of ensuring equality and inclusion for individuals with disabilities. Addressing the challenges associated with accessible parking requires a multi-faceted approach involving better design, increased enforcement, public education, and a commitment from businesses and property owners to prioritize accessibility. By working together and holding these businesses accountable, we can create a more accessible, equitable, and inclusive parking environment that benefits everyone in our communities.

Public Transportation: A Bumpy Ride

Public transportation for handicapped people can often be a "bumpy ride" due to a range of challenges and obstacles that individuals with disabilities encounter while using these services. While there have been significant improvements in accessibility in many public transportation systems, there is still much work to be done to ensure a truly inclusive and smooth experience for all passengers.

One of the primary challenges is the physical accessibility of public transportation vehicles. Buses, trains, and trams may have ramps or lifts, but these mechanisms can be prone to malfunctions or may not be maintained properly. When these accessibility features don't work as intended, it can leave wheelchair users stranded, causing frustration and inconvenience.

Moreover, the design of some public transportation vehicles can pose difficulties. Narrow aisles, inadequate space for wheelchairs, and seating configurations that don't accommodate mobility aids can make navigation within the vehicle a challenging task for passengers with disabilities. This can also result in delays as passengers struggle to board or exit the vehicle.

Infrastructure-related issues can also contribute to the "bumpy ride" of public transportation for handicapped people. Inadequate maintenance of stations or bus stops, lack of accessible signage, and poorly designed platforms can hinder accessibility. Uneven surfaces, broken elevators, and gaps between platforms and vehicles can create physical barriers and make boarding or alighting from public transportation vehicles difficult and sometimes dangerous.

Another significant concern is the attitude and behavior of fellow passengers and transportation staff. Individuals with disabilities may face discrimination, stigmatization, or a lack of assistance from other passengers. Public transportation staff may not always receive proper training on how to assist passengers with disabilities, leading to misunderstandings or mistreatment.

To improve the public transportation experience for handicapped individuals, it is essential to address these challenges comprehensively. This includes investing in well-maintained accessibility features, ensuring vehicle design considers the needs of all passengers, making infrastructure upgrades, providing sensitivity training for transportation staff, and fostering a culture of inclusivity and respect among all passengers. Only through these measures can we work towards making public transportation a smoother, more accessible, and welcoming experience for everyone.

The Quest for Accessible Restrooms

The quest for handicapped accessible restrooms is like searching for the elusive pot of gold at the end of the rainbow—except in this case, the treasure is a clean, spacious, and fully functional restroom. People with disabilities often embark on this journey with a sense of determination and a splash of humor, knowing that the quest can sometimes feel like a real-life adventure.

Picture this: you roll up to a restroom facility, optimistic that it will be accessible. As you approach, you can't help but wonder if the infamous "Out of Order" sign will rear its ugly head. But today is your lucky day! The restroom door swings open, and it's like finding a hidden oasis in a desert of inaccessible restrooms. You breathe a sigh of relief as you enter the spacious, well-designed accessible restroom. It's like finding the holy grail of bathroom experiences. At this point you might actually hear a chorus of angels singing!

Of course, not all quests have a fairy-tale ending. There are times when accessible restrooms are more elusive than a unicorn on roller skates. You may encounter restrooms with tiny stalls that seem to have been designed by someone with a fascination for phone booths from a bygone era. Or you might find restrooms that have more twists and turns than a Formula 1 racetrack, leaving you wondering if you'll ever escape.

Despite the occasional challenges and unexpected twists in the quest for handicapped accessible restrooms, the search continues. With a sense of humor, a dash of perseverance, and the support of advocates and allies, individuals with disabilities are pushing for more accessible facilities. It's a quest that may have its ups and downs, but the goal is clear: a world where accessible restrooms are not a treasure hunt but a standard part of everyday life. Until then, keep your humor intact and your restroom radar sharp—you never know when you might stumble upon that elusive accessible restroom gem, and remember, if you encounter a few rocks amidst your gleaming emerald of toilets, be sure to document them and bring it to the attention of the business owners. Many managers and employees have no stake in the game but most owners (or at least we would like to think) would prefer to be compliant due to reputation and hefty noncompliance fines.

Chapter 5: Personal Stories of Inaccessibility from Your Author

For individuals who rely on wheelchairs for mobility, navigating the world can be a challenging endeavor. While many places have improved accessibility over the years, there are still instances where wheelchair users encounter significant barriers. In this chapter, we will explore three different places that turned into complete nightmares when my husband and myself both tried to navigate them with a wheelchair.

1. IP Casino and Hotel in Biloxi, Mississippi

My husband and I were excited about a trip to the IP Casino in Biloxi, Mississippi. Our anticipation for a relaxing getaway, however, took an unexpected turn when we encountered a series of accessibility challenges that left us feeling vulnerable and frustrated.

Upon arriving at the casino, we were disheartened to discover that the only available handicap parking spots were located on the 7th floor of the parking garage. Having to navigate a crowded parking garage with cars racing up and down ramps with us less visible in wheelchairs than if we were standing up was already daunting, but what awaited us at the entrance to the elevator was even more disheartening.

The entrance to the elevator was flanked by double glass doors, a design that completely lacked handicapped access. My husband, determined to make our trip as enjoyable as possible, attempted to reach and pull open the heavy glass doors. In the process, he nearly fell out of his wheelchair, struggling to gain access for both him and me.

To our horror, when the doors eventually closed quickly behind us, they hit our chairs, causing the glass to shake ominously. We felt an overwhelming sense of vulnerability and unease as we realized that the fragile glass doors could have shattered at any moment. Stranded in the parking garage, we had to wait for a stranger to come along and offer assistance, adding an unnecessary layer of discomfort to our casino visit, not to mention the danger it put us in.

No one should feel vulnerable or unsafe while attempting to enjoy a simple evening out, and it is essential that businesses prioritize the comfort and safety of all their patrons, especially those with disabilities.

Our experience at the IP Casino in Biloxi highlights the urgent need for improved accessibility measures in public spaces. Unfortunately, that was just the beginning of what turned into a 24-hour fiasco.

Imagine checking into a hotel after an 8-hour drive, with medical equipment and with the expectation of a comfortable stay, only to find yourself trapped in your room with an incessant alarm blaring all night long. This was what we experienced after finally navigating the inaccessible garage, elevators and lobby restrooms at the IP Casino in Biloxi.

Upon realizing that the alarm was not going to be fixed anytime soon and made our room unbearable, we tried to contact the hotel staff for guidance and assistance. To our dismay, the staff not only lacked knowledge of what to do but also failed to show up to address the issue. Furthermore, the staff suggested walking down the stairs, explicitly instructing us not to use the elevator, which was an impossible task for someone using a wheelchair.

The lack of proper training and empathy in handling such situations left us feeling helpless and frustrated. This experience highlights the importance of proper disability training for staff in public establishments, ensuring that wheelchair users can enjoy their stay without unnecessary hardships.

The nightmare didn't end there. The hotel staff's inability to aid compounded the problem. After over 9 hours of this nightmare in the wee hours of the morning, we finally were able to speak with management. We informed the front desk manager of the parking garage issue, some minor problems with our room and finished our complaint to the backdrop of the still loudly clanging alarm. After she heard our concerns, she looked at us with incredulity and stated, "I'm extremely sorry but we meet the ADA <u>minimum</u> <u>requirements</u>".

That very statement is what led me to create this book. It replayed over and over in my mind. I kept seeing my husband's tired and worn face, looking at her, shocked, wondering what alternate universe we had landed in. After years of striving for excellence in the service of his country, it all boiled down to that one statement. They met the minimum requirements (supposedly) and were damn proud of it! This was a world that suddenly was totally foreign to him, even more foreign than the soil he fought a war on. In that very moment when I saw defeat on my husband's face and for so valiant a soldier to be reduced to that, I vowed to find a way to make people understand that my husband wasn't just a box on some checklist to mark, he deserved much more than the minimum requirements as do countless other disabled veterans and human beings in general. Everyone has the right to equality and dignity!

2. Southwest Airlines

Air travel is notorious for its accessibility challenges, and Southwest Airlines is no exception. Another nightmare unfolded when we decided to take a trip to the other side of the country and had to seek assistance from the airline's staff with wheelchairs and oxygen equipment in Atlanta Georgia. We found all but one staff member to be utterly clueless about accommodating our needs, despite numerous calls to the airline prior to our departure date to ensure that things went smoothly and that they were given notice as to our special circumstances.

What made matters worse was the staff's mishandling of a vital medical device—my husband's oxygen machine. Instead of providing the necessary care and support, the airline's negligence resulted in damage to the machine which destroyed it. To add insult to injury, Southwest Airlines refused to take responsibility or offer any assistance in repairing or replacing the damaged equipment after their customer service representative assured me that she was personally putting in a claim for us.

This incident underscores the critical need for better staff training and policies to ensure that wheelchair users receive the support they require when traveling by air. Airlines should prioritize passengers' safety and comfort, especially those with medical needs.

3. Helen, Georgia – A Tourist Town with Accessibility Challenges

Helen, Georgia is a charming tourist destination known for its Bavarian-inspired architecture and picturesque landscapes. However, it is also a place where wheelchair users face numerous obstacles due to limited accessibility. We are fortunate to be less than an hour away from this beautiful community, yet we are unable to enjoy it other than just driving through it on the occasional Sunday afternoon drive.

Most of the stores and restaurants in Helen have steps, narrow doorways, and crowded aisles, making them inaccessible to those in wheelchairs. This exclusionary design not only affects tourists but also the town's residents with mobility challenges.

The lack of accessibility in such a popular tourist spot is not only inconvenient but also discriminatory. Helen, like many other tourist destinations, needs to invest in making its businesses and attractions more inclusive. This would not only benefit wheelchair users but also enhance the overall visitor experience.

These three stories are just a few handpicked from many of our attempted adventures and they shed a glaringly bright light on the ongoing challenges faced by wheelchair users when trying to navigate public spaces. The experiences at the IP Casino, Southwest Airlines in Atlanta, Georgia, and the tourist destination town of Helen, Georgia, underscore the importance of promoting accessibility, adequate staff training, and empathy towards individuals with disabilities.

To create a more inclusive world, it is crucial for businesses, airlines, and tourist destinations to prioritize accessibility and ensure that wheelchair users can enjoy their experiences without encountering unnecessary nightmares. Advocacy, education, and policy changes are essential steps towards achieving this goal.

We should all strive to do more than "meet the minimum requirements" in all aspects of our lives. I, for one, refuse to settle for mediocrity. I may not be able to fix EVERYthing but I can certainly strive to improve SOME things!

If you are reading this book, I am hoping you share that same sentiment. I am also hoping that it will provide you all the information you need to join our brigade of Wheelchair Warriors and take it everywhere you go, documenting the injustices you encounter as well as complimenting those that strive to be the best of the best and genuinely care about the well being of their customers, both with disabilities no matter how big or small, and able bodied patrons as well.

Chapter 6: The Path Forward

In a nation built on the principles of equality and inclusion, it is disheartening to acknowledge that significant disability challenges continue to persist, often unnoticed or unaddressed in America. These issues can range from physical barriers to unequal treatment, and they remind us that there is still much work to be done in achieving full accessibility and inclusivity. In this chapter, we will explore some of the unaddressed disability challenges in America and the steps individuals can take to help enact change.

1. Inadequate Accessibility

Despite the Americans with Disabilities Act (ADA) being in place for over three decades, many public spaces, businesses, and even government facilities still lack adequate accessibility features as has been highlighted in the previous chapters. Wheelchair ramps may be too steep or poorly maintained, restrooms may not be fully accessible, and many buildings remain inaccessible due to architectural barriers.

What Can Be Done: Individuals can document instances of inadequate accessibility by filling out the worksheets in the back of this book and reporting their findings to the appropriate authorities. This could include taking photos or videos and sharing these findings on social media platforms with relevant hashtags to raise awareness. Additionally, organizations advocating for disability rights can play a crucial role in pressuring businesses and government entities to comply with ADA regulations.

2. Employment Discrimination

Disability-related employment discrimination remains a pervasive issue in America. Many qualified individuals with disabilities face challenges securing and retaining jobs due to biases and stigmas. This results in a significant employment gap between disabled and non-disabled individuals.

What Can Be Done: Documenting instances of employment discrimination and sharing these stories on social media can help shed light on this issue. Encouraging businesses to adopt inclusive hiring practices, providing reasonable accommodations, and promoting disability awareness in the workplace are essential steps to address this challenge.

3. Healthcare Disparities

Access to quality healthcare services for individuals with disabilities can be challenging. Disparities in healthcare can include difficulty finding accessible healthcare facilities, insurance discrimination, and inadequate support for individuals with chronic health conditions. Believe it or not, some of the most inaccessible places my husband and myself have encountered have been in hospitals and Doctor's offices. They of all people should know better and have no excuse!

What Can Be Done: Advocacy organizations can work to raise awareness of healthcare disparities and advocate for policy changes that improve access to quality healthcare services. Individuals can share their experiences with healthcare disparities on social media, encouraging lawmakers and healthcare providers to address these issues urgently.

4. Educational Barriers

Children and adults with disabilities often face barriers to accessing quality education. This can include inadequate special education services, bullying, and exclusion from extracurricular activities.

What Can Be Done: Parents, educators, and advocates can document instances of educational barriers and share these stories to push for systemic change. Collaboration with local school districts and participation in advocacy campaigns can help address these challenges.

While America has made significant strides in promoting disability rights and accessibility, many challenges persist. It is crucial for individuals to document instances of injustice and turn their findings over to the proper authorities. Equally important is the power of social media in raising awareness and putting pressure on businesses and institutions to comply with disability rights and regulations.

By working together, we can help create a more inclusive and equitable society where individuals with disabilities are not only protected by laws but also fully embraced and supported in all aspects of life. It is our collective responsibility to ensure that no one is left behind, and together we can make progress toward a more accessible and inclusive America.

The Call to Action for a More Accessible World

Are you ready to take a stand for a more inclusive and respectful world for wheelchair users? The time for change is now, and your voice is a powerful force in the battle for justice. Let's join forces as Wheelchair Warriors and work together to ensure that every aspect of life is accessible to all, regardless of mobility challenges. Here's how you can make a difference:

1. Fill Out Worksheets:

Start by filling out accessibility worksheets. These valuable tools help document instances of inaccessibility in your community. Whether it's a lack of ramps, inadequate restroom facilities, or discriminatory treatment, your experiences matter. By putting your experiences on paper, you create a tangible record of the issues that need attention.

2. Join the Wheelchair Warriors:

Connect with advocacy groups and organizations dedicated to disability rights and accessibility. Joining the Wheelchair Warriors community gives you the opportunity to amplify your voice and join forces with like-minded individuals who are committed to making a change. Together, we are stronger, and our collective efforts can bring about real progress.

3. Raise Awareness on Social Media:

Harness the power of social media to spread awareness about disability rights and accessibility issues. Share your stories, experiences, and concerns using relevant hashtags and tag businesses and organizations that need to act. Your posts can inspire change and put pressure on those who need to make improvements.

4. Engage with Local Authorities:

Don't underestimate the impact of engaging with local authorities, businesses, and organizations. Reach out to your local government representatives, city planners, and business owners to discuss accessibility issues in your community. Share your worksheets and personal stories to illustrate the importance of change.

5. Advocate for Policy Change:

Get involved in advocacy efforts aimed at changing policies and regulations that affect people with disabilities. Attend town hall meetings, participate in public hearings, and support disability-friendly legislation. Your advocacy can influence decision-makers to prioritize accessibility and respect for all.

6. Promote Education and Awareness:

Educate your community about the challenges faced by wheelchair users and the importance of inclusivity. Organize workshops, seminars, or awareness campaigns to promote understanding and empathy. Knowledge is a powerful tool in the fight for justice.

7. Support Inclusive Businesses:

Recognize and support businesses that prioritize accessibility and respect for individuals with disabilities. Patronize those establishments and encourage others to do the same. Positive reinforcement can incentivize businesses to improve their accessibility standards.

Together, as Wheelchair Warriors, we can make a profound impact on the world. By documenting injustices, advocating for change, and raising awareness, we can pave the way for a more accessible, inclusive, and respectful society where everyone, regardless of their mobility challenges, can live life to the fullest. Join us today and be a part of this important movement for justice and equality. Together, we will build a world where respect and accessibility are rights, not privileges.

On the following pages I have put together a comprehensive list of different agencies that can assist you in your cause. I purposefully did not include phone numbers because I know that most change on a frequent basis. However, a quick internet search with the name of these organizations should yield you a contact number or address rather easily.

A Personal Note to my Readers:

When you buy a new car and are getting ready to leave the car lot, what is one of the first things that you reach for?

For me it has always been that owner's manual.

I may already know almost everything that is in that car before I buy it, but I want to know the placement of all the important parts that I might need to utilize. I want to know all the bells and whistles that will make my drive more enjoyable.

This is what I want The Wheelchair Warrior's Bible to be for you. It is the manual for your daily mode of transport. I want you to keep it with you in your wheelchair, on your rollator walker or your power mobility scooter. I want it to enrich your current journey as well as future ones. You are not dependent on the kindness of strangers; you are capable of creating the change you need in this world.

Join us and countless other Wheelchair Warriors around the world in making a difference. We can win this war with a united front, one battle at a time.

Thank you so much,

Tammy Brown

1. **American Association of People with Disabilities (AAPD)**
   - Website: https://www.aapd.com/
2. **National Council on Disability (NCD)**
   - Website: https://ncd.gov/
3. **National Organization on Disability (NOD)**
   - Website: https://www.nod.org/
4. **Disability Rights Education & Defense Fund (DREDF)**
   - Website: https://dredf.org/
5. **United Spinal Association**
   - Website: https://www.unitedspinal.org/
6. **The Arc**
   - Website: https://thearc.org/
7. **Easterseals**
   - Website: https://www.easterseals.com/
8. **National Down Syndrome Society (NDSS)**
   - Website: https://www.ndss.org/
9. **Autism Speaks**
   - Website: https://www.autismspeaks.org/
10. **World Institute on Disability (WID)**
    - Website: https://wid.org/
11. **International Disability Alliance (IDA)**
    - Website: https://www.internationaldisabilityalliance.org/
12. **Disabled American Veterans (DAV)**

- Website: https://www.dav.org/

13.   **Cerebral Palsy Foundation**
   - Website: https://www.yourcpf.org/
14.   **Spina Bifida Association**
   - Website:
      https://www.spinabifidaassociation.org/
15.   **Muscular Dystrophy Association (MDA)**
   - Website: https://www.mda.org/

To get the most up-to-date contact information for these organizations, please visit their respective websites or use a search engine to find the contact details you need. Additionally, consider reaching out to local disability advocacy groups and organizations specific to your area, as they may be able to provide valuable resources and support tailored to your needs and location.

WHEELCHAIR WARRIORS' WORKSHEET

NAME OF AGENCY/BUSINESS:

_____

Area(s) Observed:_____**Date:**_____

Employee Contact Information

Business Address

Owner Contact Information

Was Business ADA compliant?

What, If Any, Problems Did you Encounter?

Were your concerns heard & addressed properly?

Did you feel discriminated against or overlooked?

In what ways can this business improve to accommodate disabled individuals better?

Please fill in any additional pertinent information below:

WHEELCHAIR WARRIORS' WORKSHEET

NAME OF AGENCY/BUSINESS:

Area(s) Observed:_____**Date:**_____

Employee Contact Information

Business Address

Owner Contact Information

Was Business ADA compliant?

What, If Any, Problems Did you Encounter?

Were your concerns heard & addressed properly?

Did you feel discriminated against or overlooked?

In what ways can this business improve to accommodate disabled individuals better?

Please fill in any additional pertinent information below:

WHEELCHAIR WARRIORS' WORKSHEET

NAME OF AGENCY/BUSINESS:

_____

Area(s) Observed:_____**Date:**_____

Employee Contact Information

Business Address

Owner Contact Information

Was Business ADA compliant?

What, If Any, Problems Did you Encounter?

Were your concerns heard & addressed properly?

Did you feel discriminated against or overlooked?

In what ways can this business improve to accommodate disabled individuals better?

Please fill in any additional pertinent information below:

WHEELCHAIR WARRIORS' WORKSHEET

NAME OF AGENCY/BUSINESS:

_____

Area(s) Observed:_____**Date:**_____

Employee Contact Information

Business Address

Owner Contact Information

Was Business ADA compliant?

What, If Any, Problems Did you Encounter?

Were your concerns heard & addressed properly?

Did you feel discriminated against or overlooked?

In what ways can this business improve to accommodate disabled individuals better?

Please fill in any additional pertinent information below:

WHEELCHAIR WARRIORS' WORKSHEET

NAME OF AGENCY/BUSINESS:

Area(s) Observed:_____**Date:**_____

Employee Contact Information

Business Address

Owner Contact Information

Was Business ADA compliant?

What, If Any, Problems Did you Encounter?

Were your concerns heard & addressed properly?

Did you feel discriminated against or overlooked?

In what ways can this business improve to accommodate disabled individuals better?

Please fill in any additional pertinent information below:

WHEELCHAIR WARRIORS' WORKSHEET

NAME OF AGENCY/BUSINESS:

Area(s) Observed:_____**Date:**_____

Employee Contact Information

Business Address

Owner Contact Information

Was Business ADA compliant?

What, If Any, Problems Did you Encounter?

Were your concerns heard & addressed properly?

Did you feel discriminated against or overlooked?

In what ways can this business improve to accommodate disabled individuals better?

Please fill in any additional pertinent information below:

WHEELCHAIR WARRIORS' WORKSHEET

NAME OF AGENCY/BUSINESS:

Area(s) Observed:_____**Date:**_____

Employee Contact Information

Business Address

Owner Contact Information

Was Business ADA compliant?

What, If Any, Problems Did you Encounter?

Were your concerns heard & addressed properly?

Did you feel discriminated against or overlooked?

In what ways can this business improve to accommodate disabled individuals better?

Please fill in any additional pertinent information below:

WHEELCHAIR WARRIORS' WORKSHEET

NAME OF AGENCY/BUSINESS:

Area(s) Observed:_____**Date:**_____

Employee Contact Information

Business Address

Owner Contact Information

Was Business ADA compliant?

What, If Any, Problems Did you Encounter?

Were your concerns heard & addressed properly?

Did you feel discriminated against or overlooked?

In what ways can this business improve to accommodate disabled individuals better?

Please fill in any additional pertinent information below:

WHEELCHAIR WARRIORS' WORKSHEET

NAME OF AGENCY/BUSINESS:

Area(s) Observed:_____**Date:**_____

Employee Contact Information

Business Address

Owner Contact Information

Was Business ADA compliant?

What, If Any, Problems Did you Encounter?

Were your concerns heard & addressed properly?

Did you feel discriminated against or overlooked?

In what ways can this business improve to accommodate disabled individuals better?

Please fill in any additional pertinent information below:

WHEELCHAIR WARRIORS' WORKSHEET

NAME OF AGENCY/BUSINESS:

Area(s) Observed:_____**Date:**_____

Employee Contact Information

Business Address

Owner Contact Information

Was Business ADA compliant?

What, If Any, Problems Did you Encounter?

Were your concerns heard & addressed properly?

Did you feel discriminated against or overlooked?

In what ways can this business improve to accommodate disabled individuals better?

Please fill in any additional pertinent information below:

WHEELCHAIR WARRIORS' WORKSHEET

NAME OF AGENCY/BUSINESS:

Area(s) Observed:_____**Date:**_____

Employee Contact Information

Business Address

Owner Contact Information

Was Business ADA compliant?

What, If Any, Problems Did you Encounter?

Were your concerns heard & addressed properly?

Did you feel discriminated against or overlooked?

In what ways can this business improve to accommodate disabled individuals better?

Please fill in any additional pertinent information below:

WHEELCHAIR WARRIORS' WORKSHEET

NAME OF AGENCY/BUSINESS:

_____

Area(s) Observed:_____**Date:**_____

Employee Contact Information

Business Address

Owner Contact Information

Was Business ADA compliant?

What, If Any, Problems Did you Encounter?

Were your concerns heard & addressed properly?

Did you feel discriminated against or overlooked?

In what ways can this business improve to accommodate disabled individuals better?

Please fill in any additional pertinent information below:

WHEELCHAIR WARRIORS' WORKSHEET

NAME OF AGENCY/BUSINESS:
_____

Area(s) Observed:_____**Date:**_____

Employee Contact Information

Business Address

Owner Contact Information

Was Business ADA compliant?

What, If Any, Problems Did you Encounter?

Were your concerns heard & addressed properly?

Did you feel discriminated against or overlooked?

In what ways can this business improve to accommodate disabled individuals better?

Please fill in any additional pertinent information below:

WHEELCHAIR WARRIORS' WORKSHEET

NAME OF AGENCY/BUSINESS:

_____

Area(s) Observed:_____**Date:**_____

Employee Contact Information

Business Address

Owner Contact Information

Was Business ADA compliant?

What, If Any, Problems Did you Encounter?

Were your concerns heard & addressed properly?

Did you feel discriminated against or overlooked?

In what ways can this business improve to accommodate disabled individuals better?

Please fill in any additional pertinent information below:

WHEELCHAIR WARRIORS' WORKSHEET

NAME OF AGENCY/BUSINESS:

_____

Area(s) Observed:_____**Date:**_____

Employee Contact Information

Business Address

Owner Contact Information

Was Business ADA compliant?

What, If Any, Problems Did you Encounter?

Were your concerns heard & addressed properly?

Did you feel discriminated against or overlooked?

In what ways can this business improve to accommodate disabled individuals better?

Please fill in any additional pertinent information below:

WHEELCHAIR WARRIORS' WORKSHEET

NAME OF AGENCY/BUSINESS:

Area(s) Observed:_____**Date:**_____

Employee Contact Information

Business Address

Owner Contact Information

Was Business ADA compliant?

What, If Any, Problems Did you Encounter?

Were your concerns heard & addressed properly?

Did you feel discriminated against or overlooked?

In what ways can this business improve to accommodate disabled individuals better?

Please fill in any additional pertinent information below:

WHEELCHAIR WARRIORS' WORKSHEET

NAME OF AGENCY/BUSINESS:

Area(s) Observed:_____**Date:**_____

Employee Contact Information

Business Address

Owner Contact Information

Was Business ADA compliant?

What, If Any, Problems Did you Encounter?

Were your concerns heard & addressed properly?

Did you feel discriminated against or overlooked?

In what ways can this business improve to accommodate disabled individuals better?

Please fill in any additional pertinent information below:

WHEELCHAIR WARRIORS' WORKSHEET

NAME OF AGENCY/BUSINESS:

_____

Area(s) Observed:_____**Date:**_____

Employee Contact Information

Business Address

Owner Contact Information

Was Business ADA compliant?

What, If Any, Problems Did you Encounter?

Were your concerns heard & addressed properly?

Did you feel discriminated against or overlooked?

In what ways can this business improve to accommodate disabled individuals better?

Please fill in any additional pertinent information below:

WHEELCHAIR WARRIORS' WORKSHEET

NAME OF AGENCY/BUSINESS:

Area(s) Observed:_____**Date:**_____

Employee Contact Information

Business Address

Owner Contact Information

Was Business ADA compliant?

What, If Any, Problems Did you Encounter?

Were your concerns heard & addressed properly?

Did you feel discriminated against or overlooked?

In what ways can this business improve to accommodate disabled individuals better?

Please fill in any additional pertinent information below:

WHEELCHAIR WARRIORS' WORKSHEET

NAME OF AGENCY/BUSINESS:

Area(s) Observed:_____**Date:**_____

Employee Contact Information

Business Address

Owner Contact Information

Was Business ADA compliant?

What, If Any, Problems Did you Encounter?

Were your concerns heard & addressed properly?

Did you feel discriminated against or overlooked?

In what ways can this business improve to accommodate disabled individuals better?

Please fill in any additional pertinent information below:

WHEELCHAIR WARRIORS' WORKSHEET

NAME OF AGENCY/BUSINESS:

_____

Area(s) Observed:_____**Date:**_____

Employee Contact Information

Business Address

Owner Contact Information

Was Business ADA compliant?

What, If Any, Problems Did you Encounter?

Were your concerns heard & addressed properly?

Did you feel discriminated against or overlooked?

In what ways can this business improve to accommodate disabled individuals better?

Please fill in any additional pertinent information below:

WHEELCHAIR WARRIORS' WORKSHEET

NAME OF AGENCY/BUSINESS:

Area(s) Observed:_____**Date:**_____

Employee Contact Information

Business Address

Owner Contact Information

Was Business ADA compliant?

What, If Any, Problems Did you Encounter?

Were your concerns heard & addressed properly?

Did you feel discriminated against or overlooked?

In what ways can this business improve to accommodate disabled individuals better?

Please fill in any additional pertinent information below:

WHEELCHAIR WARRIORS' WORKSHEET

NAME OF AGENCY/BUSINESS:

_____

Area(s) Observed:_____**Date:**_____

Employee Contact Information

Business Address

Owner Contact Information

Was Business ADA compliant?

What, If Any, Problems Did you Encounter?

Were your concerns heard & addressed properly?

Did you feel discriminated against or overlooked?

In what ways can this business improve to accommodate disabled individuals better?

Please fill in any additional pertinent information below:

WHEELCHAIR WARRIORS' WORKSHEET

NAME OF AGENCY/BUSINESS:

_____

Area(s) Observed:_____**Date:**_____

Employee Contact Information

Business Address

Owner Contact Information

Was Business ADA compliant?

What, If Any, Problems Did you Encounter?

Were your concerns heard & addressed properly?

Did you feel discriminated against or overlooked?

In what ways can this business improve to accommodate disabled individuals better?

Please fill in any additional pertinent information below:

WHEELCHAIR WARRIORS' WORKSHEET

NAME OF AGENCY/BUSINESS:

_____

Area(s) Observed:_____**Date:**_____

Employee Contact Information

Business Address

Owner Contact Information

Was Business ADA compliant?

What, If Any, Problems Did you Encounter?

Were your concerns heard & addressed properly?

Did you feel discriminated against or overlooked?

In what ways can this business improve to accommodate disabled individuals better?

Please fill in any additional pertinent information below:

WHEELCHAIR WARRIORS' WORKSHEET

NAME OF AGENCY/BUSINESS:

Area(s) Observed:_____**Date:**_____

Employee Contact Information

Business Address

Owner Contact Information

Was Business ADA compliant?

What, If Any, Problems Did you Encounter?

Were your concerns heard & addressed properly?

Did you feel discriminated against or overlooked?

In what ways can this business improve to accommodate disabled individuals better?

Please fill in any additional pertinent information below:

WHEELCHAIR WARRIORS' WORKSHEET

NAME OF AGENCY/BUSINESS:

Area(s) Observed:_____Date:_____

Employee Contact Information

Business Address

Owner Contact Information

Was Business ADA compliant?

What, If Any, Problems Did you Encounter?

Were your concerns heard & addressed properly?

Did you feel discriminated against or overlooked?

In what ways can this business improve to accommodate disabled individuals better?

Please fill in any additional pertinent information below:

WHEELCHAIR WARRIORS' WORKSHEET

NAME OF AGENCY/BUSINESS:

_____

Area(s) Observed:_____**Date:**_____

Employee Contact Information

Business Address

Owner Contact Information

Was Business ADA compliant?

What, If Any, Problems Did you Encounter?

Were your concerns heard & addressed properly?

Did you feel discriminated against or overlooked?

In what ways can this business improve to accommodate disabled individuals better?

Please fill in any additional pertinent information below:

WHEELCHAIR WARRIORS' WORKSHEET

NAME OF AGENCY/BUSINESS:

_____

Area(s) Observed:_____**Date:**_____

Employee Contact Information

Business Address

Owner Contact Information

Was Business ADA compliant?

What, If Any, Problems Did you Encounter?

Were your concerns heard & addressed properly?

Did you feel discriminated against or overlooked?

In what ways can this business improve to accommodate disabled individuals better?

Please fill in any additional pertinent information below:

WHEELCHAIR WARRIORS' WORKSHEET

NAME OF AGENCY/BUSINESS:

_____

Area(s) Observed:_____**Date:**_____

Employee Contact Information

Business Address

Owner Contact Information

Was Business ADA compliant?

What, If Any, Problems Did you Encounter?

Were your concerns heard & addressed properly?

Did you feel discriminated against or overlooked?

In what ways can this business improve to accommodate disabled individuals better?

Please fill in any additional pertinent information below:

WHEELCHAIR WARRIORS' WORKSHEET

NAME OF AGENCY/BUSINESS:

_____

Area(s) Observed:_____**Date:**_____

Employee Contact Information

Business Address

Owner Contact Information

Was Business ADA compliant?

What, If Any, Problems Did you Encounter?

Were your concerns heard & addressed properly?

Did you feel discriminated against or overlooked?

In what ways can this business improve to accommodate disabled individuals better?

Please fill in any additional pertinent information below:

WHEELCHAIR WARRIORS' WORKSHEET

NAME OF AGENCY/BUSINESS:

Area(s) Observed:_____**Date:**_____

Employee Contact Information

Business Address

Owner Contact Information

Was Business ADA compliant?

What, If Any, Problems Did you Encounter?

Were your concerns heard & addressed properly?

Did you feel discriminated against or overlooked?

In what ways can this business improve to accommodate disabled individuals better?

Please fill in any additional pertinent information below:

WHEELCHAIR WARRIORS' WORKSHEET

NAME OF AGENCY/BUSINESS:

_____

Area(s) Observed:_____**Date:**_____

Employee Contact Information

Business Address

Owner Contact Information

Was Business ADA compliant?

What, If Any, Problems Did you Encounter?

Were your concerns heard & addressed properly?

Did you feel discriminated against or overlooked?

In what ways can this business improve to accommodate disabled individuals better?

Please fill in any additional pertinent information below:

WHEELCHAIR WARRIORS' WORKSHEET

NAME OF AGENCY/BUSINESS:

Area(s) Observed:_____**Date:**_____

Employee Contact Information

Business Address

Owner Contact Information

Was Business ADA compliant?

What, If Any, Problems Did you Encounter?

Were your concerns heard & addressed properly?

Did you feel discriminated against or overlooked?

In what ways can this business improve to accommodate disabled individuals better?

Please fill in any additional pertinent information below:

WHEELCHAIR WARRIORS' WORKSHEET

NAME OF AGENCY/BUSINESS:
_____

Area(s) Observed:_____**Date:**_____

Employee Contact Information

Business Address

Owner Contact Information

Was Business ADA compliant?

What, If Any, Problems Did you Encounter?

Were your concerns heard & addressed properly?

Did you feel discriminated against or overlooked?

In what ways can this business improve to accommodate disabled individuals better?

Please fill in any additional pertinent information below:

WHEELCHAIR WARRIORS' WORKSHEET

NAME OF AGENCY/BUSINESS:

_____

Area(s) Observed:_____**Date:**_____

Employee Contact Information

Business Address

Owner Contact Information

Was Business ADA compliant?

What, If Any, Problems Did you Encounter?

Were your concerns heard & addressed properly?

Did you feel discriminated against or overlooked?

In what ways can this business improve to accommodate disabled individuals better?

Please fill in any additional pertinent information below:

WHEELCHAIR WARRIORS' WORKSHEET

NAME OF AGENCY/BUSINESS:
_____

Area(s) Observed:_____**Date:**_____

Employee Contact Information

Business Address

Owner Contact Information

Was Business ADA compliant?

What, If Any, Problems Did you Encounter?

Were your concerns heard & addressed properly?

Did you feel discriminated against or overlooked?

In what ways can this business improve to accommodate disabled individuals better?

Please fill in any additional pertinent information below:

WHEELCHAIR WARRIORS' WORKSHEET

NAME OF AGENCY/BUSINESS:

Area(s) Observed:_____**Date:**_____

Employee Contact Information

Business Address

Owner Contact Information

Was Business ADA compliant?

What, If Any, Problems Did you Encounter?

Were your concerns heard & addressed properly?

Did you feel discriminated against or overlooked?

In what ways can this business improve to accommodate disabled individuals better?

Please fill in any additional pertinent information below:

WHEELCHAIR WARRIORS' WORKSHEET

NAME OF AGENCY/BUSINESS:

_____

Area(s) Observed:_____**Date:**_____

Employee Contact Information

Business Address

Owner Contact Information

Was Business ADA compliant?

What, If Any, Problems Did you Encounter?

Were your concerns heard & addressed properly?

Did you feel discriminated against or overlooked?

In what ways can this business improve to accommodate disabled individuals better?

Please fill in any additional pertinent information below:

WHEELCHAIR WARRIORS' WORKSHEET

NAME OF AGENCY/BUSINESS:

Area(s) Observed:_____**Date:**_____

Employee Contact Information

Business Address

Owner Contact Information

Was Business ADA compliant?

What, If Any, Problems Did you Encounter?

Were your concerns heard & addressed properly?

Did you feel discriminated against or overlooked?

In what ways can this business improve to accommodate disabled individuals better?

Please fill in any additional pertinent information below:

WHEELCHAIR WARRIORS' WORKSHEET

NAME OF AGENCY/BUSINESS:

_____

Area(s) Observed:_____**Date:**_____

Employee Contact Information

Business Address

Owner Contact Information

Was Business ADA compliant?

What, If Any, Problems Did you Encounter?

Were your concerns heard & addressed properly?

Did you feel discriminated against or overlooked?

In what ways can this business improve to accommodate disabled individuals better?

Please fill in any additional pertinent information below:

WHEELCHAIR WARRIORS' WORKSHEET

NAME OF AGENCY/BUSINESS:

_____

Area(s) Observed:_____**Date:**_____

Employee Contact Information

Business Address

Owner Contact Information

Was Business ADA compliant?

What, If Any, Problems Did you Encounter?

Were your concerns heard & addressed properly?

Did you feel discriminated against or overlooked?

In what ways can this business improve to accommodate disabled individuals better?

Please fill in any additional pertinent information below:

WHEELCHAIR WARRIORS' WORKSHEET

NAME OF AGENCY/BUSINESS:

_____

Area(s) Observed:_____**Date:**_____

Employee Contact Information

Business Address

Owner Contact Information

Was Business ADA compliant?

What, If Any, Problems Did you Encounter?

Were your concerns heard & addressed properly?

Did you feel discriminated against or overlooked?

In what ways can this business improve to accommodate disabled individuals better?

Please fill in any additional pertinent information below:

WHEELCHAIR WARRIORS' WORKSHEET

NAME OF AGENCY/BUSINESS:

Area(s) Observed:_____**Date:**_____

Employee Contact Information

Business Address

Owner Contact Information

Was Business ADA compliant?

What, If Any, Problems Did you Encounter?

Were your concerns heard & addressed properly?

Did you feel discriminated against or overlooked?

In what ways can this business improve to accommodate disabled individuals better?

Please fill in any additional pertinent information below:

WHEELCHAIR WARRIORS' WORKSHEET

NAME OF AGENCY/BUSINESS:

Area(s) Observed:_____**Date:**_____

Employee Contact Information

Business Address

Owner Contact Information

Was Business ADA compliant?

What, If Any, Problems Did you Encounter?

Were your concerns heard & addressed properly?

Did you feel discriminated against or overlooked?

In what ways can this business improve to accommodate disabled individuals better?

Please fill in any additional pertinent information below:

WHEELCHAIR WARRIORS' WORKSHEET

NAME OF AGENCY/BUSINESS:

_____

Area(s) Observed:_____**Date:**_____

Employee Contact Information

Business Address

Owner Contact Information

Was Business ADA compliant?

What, If Any, Problems Did you Encounter?

Were your concerns heard & addressed properly?

Did you feel discriminated against or overlooked?

In what ways can this business improve to accommodate disabled individuals better?

Please fill in any additional pertinent information below:

WHEELCHAIR WARRIORS' WORKSHEET

NAME OF AGENCY/BUSINESS:

_____

Area(s) Observed:_____**Date:**_____

Employee Contact Information

Business Address

Owner Contact Information

Was Business ADA compliant?

What, If Any, Problems Did you Encounter?

Were your concerns heard & addressed properly?

Did you feel discriminated against or overlooked?

In what ways can this business improve to accommodate disabled individuals better?

Please fill in any additional pertinent information below:

WHEELCHAIR WARRIORS' WORKSHEET

NAME OF AGENCY/BUSINESS:

_____

Area(s) Observed:_____**Date:**_____

Employee Contact Information

Business Address

Owner Contact Information

Was Business ADA compliant?

What, If Any, Problems Did you Encounter?

Were your concerns heard & addressed properly?

Did you feel discriminated against or overlooked?

In what ways can this business improve to accommodate disabled individuals better?

Please fill in any additional pertinent information below:

WHEELCHAIR WARRIORS' WORKSHEET

NAME OF AGENCY/BUSINESS:

_____

Area(s) Observed:_____**Date:**_____

Employee Contact Information

Business Address

Owner Contact Information

Was Business ADA compliant?

What, If Any, Problems Did you Encounter?

Were your concerns heard & addressed properly?

Did you feel discriminated against or overlooked?

In what ways can this business improve to accommodate disabled individuals better?

Please fill in any additional pertinent information below:

WHEELCHAIR WARRIORS' WORKSHEET

NAME OF AGENCY/BUSINESS:

Area(s) Observed:_____Date:_____

Employee Contact Information

Business Address

Owner Contact Information

Was Business ADA compliant?

What, If Any, Problems Did you Encounter?

Were your concerns heard & addressed properly?

Did you feel discriminated against or overlooked?

In what ways can this business improve to accommodate disabled individuals better?

Please fill in any additional pertinent information below:

WHEELCHAIR WARRIORS' WORKSHEET

NAME OF AGENCY/BUSINESS:

_____

Area(s) Observed:_____**Date:**_____

Employee Contact Information

Business Address

Owner Contact Information

Was Business ADA compliant?

What, If Any, Problems Did you Encounter?

Were your concerns heard & addressed properly?

Did you feel discriminated against or overlooked?

In what ways can this business improve to accommodate disabled individuals better?

Please fill in any additional pertinent information below:

WHEELCHAIR WARRIORS' WORKSHEET

NAME OF AGENCY/BUSINESS:

_____

Area(s) Observed:_____**Date:**_____

Employee Contact Information

Business Address

Owner Contact Information

Was Business ADA compliant?

What, If Any, Problems Did you Encounter?

Were your concerns heard & addressed properly?

Did you feel discriminated against or overlooked?

In what ways can this business improve to accommodate disabled individuals better?

Please fill in any additional pertinent information below:

WHEELCHAIR WARRIORS' WORKSHEET

NAME OF AGENCY/BUSINESS:

_____

Area(s) Observed:_____**Date:**_____

Employee Contact Information

Business Address

Owner Contact Information

Was Business ADA compliant?

What, If Any, Problems Did you Encounter?

Were your concerns heard & addressed properly?

Did you feel discriminated against or overlooked?

In what ways can this business improve to accommodate disabled individuals better?

Please fill in any additional pertinent information below:

WHEELCHAIR WARRIORS' WORKSHEET

NAME OF AGENCY/BUSINESS:

Area(s) Observed:_____**Date:**_____

Employee Contact Information

Business Address

Owner Contact Information

Was Business ADA compliant?

What, If Any, Problems Did you Encounter?

Were your concerns heard & addressed properly?

Did you feel discriminated against or overlooked?

In what ways can this business improve to accommodate disabled individuals better?

Please fill in any additional pertinent information below:

WHEELCHAIR WARRIORS' WORKSHEET

NAME OF AGENCY/BUSINESS:

_____

Area(s) Observed:_____**Date:**_____

Employee Contact Information

Business Address

Owner Contact Information

Was Business ADA compliant?

What, If Any, Problems Did you Encounter?

Were your concerns heard & addressed properly?

Did you feel discriminated against or overlooked?

In what ways can this business improve to accommodate disabled individuals better?

Please fill in any additional pertinent information below:

WHEELCHAIR WARRIORS' WORKSHEET

NAME OF AGENCY/BUSINESS:

_____

Area(s) Observed:_____**Date:**_____

Employee Contact Information

Business Address

Owner Contact Information

Was Business ADA compliant?

What, If Any, Problems Did you Encounter?

Were your concerns heard & addressed properly?

Did you feel discriminated against or overlooked?

In what ways can this business improve to accommodate disabled individuals better?

Please fill in any additional pertinent information below:

WHEELCHAIR WARRIORS' WORKSHEET

NAME OF AGENCY/BUSINESS:

_____

Area(s) Observed:_____**Date:**_____

Employee Contact Information

Business Address

Owner Contact Information

Was Business ADA compliant?

What, If Any, Problems Did you Encounter?

Were your concerns heard & addressed properly?

Did you feel discriminated against or overlooked?

In what ways can this business improve to accommodate disabled individuals better?

Please fill in any additional pertinent information below:

WHEELCHAIR WARRIORS' WORKSHEET

NAME OF AGENCY/BUSINESS:
_____

Area(s) Observed:_____**Date:**_____

Employee Contact Information

Business Address

Owner Contact Information

Was Business ADA compliant?

What, If Any, Problems Did you Encounter?

Were your concerns heard & addressed properly?

Did you feel discriminated against or overlooked?

In what ways can this business improve to accommodate disabled individuals better?

Please fill in any additional pertinent information below:

WHEELCHAIR WARRIORS' WORKSHEET

NAME OF AGENCY/BUSINESS:

Area(s) Observed:_____Date:_____

Employee Contact Information

Business Address

Owner Contact Information

Was Business ADA compliant?

What, If Any, Problems Did you Encounter?

Were your concerns heard & addressed properly?

Did you feel discriminated against or overlooked?

In what ways can this business improve to accommodate disabled individuals better?

Please fill in any additional pertinent information below:

WHEELCHAIR WARRIORS' WORKSHEET

NAME OF AGENCY/BUSINESS:

_____

Area(s) Observed:_____**Date:**_____

Employee Contact Information

Business Address

Owner Contact Information

Was Business ADA compliant?

What, If Any, Problems Did you Encounter?

Were your concerns heard & addressed properly?

Did you feel discriminated against or overlooked?

In what ways can this business improve to accommodate disabled individuals better?

Please fill in any additional pertinent information below:

WHEELCHAIR WARRIORS' WORKSHEET

NAME OF AGENCY/BUSINESS:

Area(s) Observed:_____**Date:**_____

Employee Contact Information

Business Address

Owner Contact Information

Was Business ADA compliant?

What, If Any, Problems Did you Encounter?

Were your concerns heard & addressed properly?

Did you feel discriminated against or overlooked?

In what ways can this business improve to accommodate disabled individuals better?

Please fill in any additional pertinent information below:

WHEELCHAIR WARRIORS' WORKSHEET

NAME OF AGENCY/BUSINESS:

_____

Area(s) Observed:_____**Date:**_____

Employee Contact Information

Business Address

Owner Contact Information

Was Business ADA compliant?

What, If Any, Problems Did you Encounter?

Were your concerns heard & addressed properly?

Did you feel discriminated against or overlooked?

In what ways can this business improve to accommodate disabled individuals better?

Please fill in any additional pertinent information below:

WHEELCHAIR WARRIORS' WORKSHEET

NAME OF AGENCY/BUSINESS:

_____

Area(s) Observed:_____**Date:**_____

Employee Contact Information

Business Address

Owner Contact Information

Was Business ADA compliant?

What, If Any, Problems Did you Encounter?

Were your concerns heard & addressed properly?

Did you feel discriminated against or overlooked?

In what ways can this business improve to accommodate disabled individuals better?

Please fill in any additional pertinent information below:

WHEELCHAIR WARRIORS' WORKSHEET

NAME OF AGENCY/BUSINESS:

Area(s) Observed:_____Date:_____

Employee Contact Information

Business Address

Owner Contact Information

Was Business ADA compliant?

What, If Any, Problems Did you Encounter?

Were your concerns heard & addressed properly?

Did you feel discriminated against or overlooked?

In what ways can this business improve to accommodate disabled individuals better?

Please fill in any additional pertinent information below:

ABOUT THE AUTHOR

Introducing the Wheelchair Warrior behind this informative call to action book. Meet the talented author, Tammy L Brown, born in the city of Louisville, Kentucky. She now calls the picturesque town of Toccoa, Georgia, her home. As a loving mother of four and a proud grandmother to ten precious little ones, she has always cherished the joy of storytelling and spending time with her family.